A Beginner's Guide to Storytelling

A Nati  **Guide**

Editor
Katy Rydell

Graphic Designer
Karen Wollscheid

Produced under the direction of
Glenn Morrow
NSN Board Liaison and
Chair, Communications Committee
and
the National Storytelling Press Committee
Jill Johnson
Joan Kimball
Barbara Schutzgruber
Judy Sima

National Storytelling Press
a division of
National Storytelling Network

NATIONAL
STORYTELLING
NETWORK

ISBN: 1-879991-32-2

Published by
National Storytelling Press

Distributed by
National Storytelling Network
132 Boone Street
Jonesborough TN 37659
Toll Free: 1-800-525-4514
Direct: 423-913-8201
E-mail: nsn@storynet.org
Website: www.storynet.org

Table of Contents

Welcome

Everything has a beginning. Every journey begins with a first step. Except in stories, where, as Joseph Campbell says, before the first step is taken, the hero's quest begins with an invitation. So you might think of this as your invitation to begin a journey into the world of storytelling.

Once that invitation has been offered, the hero of your story must venture forth. Whether by dint of luck and pluck, good advice, or the promise of help from faithful companions, the success of the journey depends on the hero's willingness to screw up his courage and take that first step. Do it!! As the great Sufi poet, Kabir says, the journey is everything, the destination unimportant.

Wait, you say, I am unprepared. I have so many questions needing an answer before I can begin.

There's no getting around the fact that everyone who claims to be a storyteller had to answer the same questions you do. It's true. Donald Davis had to learn how to tell a story. So did Augusta Baker, Jackie Torrence, Ray Hicks, and Elizabeth Ellis. All of them made that first step from the desire to tell to doing the deed. All of them began with a mix of the terrible fear of failure and desire to share the experience they had of hearing a good story well told.

For many of us, learning to be a storyteller is a difficult and ongoing process of trying and failing, revising and trying again. The more you learn, the more you realize there is more to know. The better you get, the easier it is to see how much is left to learn. With enough practice and with a little help along the way, most of us find the process of identifying, crafting, and telling a story to be a worthwhile process. And for many of us, whatever help we can get to understand the how and why of storytelling is greatly appreciated.

You might think of this book as a guide. It is not a comprehensive history of the subject, for the world of storytelling is vast and you can easily spend years and a small fortune seeking that all-encompassing kind of knowledge and experience without exhausting its possibilities. Instead, you might think of this book as a pocket guide, pointing out areas of interest worth further exploration.

As a storyteller, teacher of storytelling and member of the National Storytelling Network, I hope that this book will be a welcome guide and useful tool for your exploration of all things told. The National Storytelling Network is happy to make this available and hopes that as you learn more about this most human of arts, you will want to join us in celebrating and advocating for storytelling in all its forms.

Welcome, traveler! This is a great long road we are on, and the stories you tell along the way are much appreciated.

Loren Niemi
Storyteller
Chair, NSN Board of Directors

What is NSN?

The National Storytelling Network (NSN) is a member-driven organization that offers direct services, publications and educational opportunities to several thousand individuals, local storytelling guilds and associations. These services are designed to improve the quality of storytelling at all levels – in public venues, in classrooms and libraries, and wherever storytelling can make a contribution to the quality of life. To facilitate that process NSN sponsors the National Storytelling Conference at a different location each summer. The Conference provides educational workshops, demonstration programs, an opportunity for members to tell stories before a national audience, and the National Storytelling Awards Ceremony that recognizes storytelling excellence, leadership and service across the country.

Other services offered by NSN include the website, StoryNet; *Storytelling Magazine* published 5 times a year, the bi-weekly electronic newsletter, the Bulletin, and an online directory of Teller Pages, a guide to professional storytellers.

One of NSN's most widely known programs is Tellabration! In 1988 the Connecticut Storytelling Center came up with a simple idea: on the Saturday before Thanksgiving, storytellers should gather together and tell stories. They did, in six locations across the state. Since then Tellabration! has become an international event, celebrated in more than three hundred locations around the world.

NSN's Special Interest Groups include the Healing Story Alliance, Youth Storytelling, Storytelling in Organizations, Storytelling in Higher Education, and Event/Festival Organizers. These groups offer opportunities for members to share information and provide support for those interested in and working in these areas.

Each state has a State Liaison who can provide information on local groups and contacts. Larger states have more than one Liaison. For more information about NSN and to get the name of your state representative, contact National Storytelling Network, 132 Boone Street, Jonesborough TN 37659; call 800-525-4514 or 423-913-8201; nsn@storynet.org or www.storynet.org.

Acknowledgements

This project could not have been completed without the energy and ongoing commitment of many people. NSN Executive Director Nancy Kavanaugh was the catalyst who got it started. Janice Del Negro, Flora Joy, and former board member Doug Lipman provided early input. Debra Olson Tolar helped with the editing.

As board member and Chair of the Communications Committee, Glenn Morrow was a strong advocate and an invaluable guide through the funding, design and production process.

Many thanks especially to the members of the NSN Press Committee: Jill Johnson, Barbara Schutzgruber, and Judy Sima, who generously offered ideas, advice, interest, and enthusiasm, without which this project would have been difficult to complete, and nowhere near as much fun. Thanks to Press Committee Chair Joan Kimball for what she calls her "doggedness," and what the rest of us call hard work, fine leadership, and excellent editing skills.

Katy Rydell, Editor

This book, three years in the making, began with the request of NSN Executive Director Nancy Kavanaugh to an untried Press Committee. Developing the topics, we reaped valuable advice from thirty-six members of the Storytell Listserv. Doug Lipman and Flora Joy gave us initial guidance and encouragement. Board member Glenn Morrow rescued us from a midway slowdown. Our kudos go to Katy Rydell, our editor, who came on board a year ago. Picking up the tempo, she took over the search for writers and fine-tuned our plan long before tackling the editing itself. And it has been a pleasure to work with our unflappable graphic designer, Karen Wollscheid. Special thanks also go to the authors who donated so many hours of their time. But above all, the companionship and support of my fellow committee members, Barbara Schutzgruber, Judy Sima, and Jill Johnson, has been a precious gift to me.

Joan Kimball, Chair
NSN Press Committee

Introduction

All humans tell stories. Your partner, child, or parent asks you, "Where were you yesterday?" You concoct a factual (or fanciful) account of your previous day, with a beginning, a middle, and an end. You are telling a story.

Why then do you need advice about storytelling? Perhaps you plan to tell stories to groups of people. Perhaps you want to persuade or educate or entertain a wedding party, a scout troop, a jury, or a gathering of tourists or stockholders. You need to prepare more carefully to tell to a group.

The office of the National Storytelling Network gets requests every week from people who want guidance. People ask, how do I find stories to tell? Learn a story? Use storytelling to put my ideas across? Cope with stage fright? Pace my stories? Find a coach? Use a mike?

The ability to tell to groups successfully starts with practice in friendly places, learning from both triumphs and failures. Advice can help you avoid some pitfalls and give you good techniques. One book, however, will not make you a professional teller, able to charge hundreds of dollars for a single stage performance. Professional storytelling takes many, many years of experience.

The ideas in this book, coming from a number of seasoned tellers, may sometimes appear contradictory. Life experiences don't necessarily match up. So pick the advice that matches your needs. Whatever your destination, it's our hope that reading this book will launch you in the performance, the adventure, and the fun of storytelling. Welcome aboard!

Joan Kimball, Chair
NSN Press Committee

Choosing a Story

by Gay Ducey

It seems like magic. A teller begins a tale and as it unfolds, the story and the teller seem meant for each other. It is hard to imagine anyone else telling that story. When the disparate elements of storyteller and story combine to form gold, that is part of the alchemy of storytelling. Every teller prizes that experience. Such a happy marriage can be yours as well, but not without the requisite search, courtship, and commitment. In short, not without a bit of effort.

Among the processes that accompany becoming a storyteller none is more important than choosing the story. Perversely, no other topic is more likely to engender more incomplete advice and confusing intimations of the indefinable. This is understandable, since the reality is part common sense and part mystery. Do not despair: guideposts and landmarks show the way toward finding and snaring your quarry.

Listen

Listening is where telling begins. Cooking works the same way: before we bake a fine cake, we need to know what a good cake tastes like. When we hear a good storyteller share a good story, we learn. Take your time then, and listen. Stories were meant to be experienced and remembered this way. Seek out storytellers performing before a live audience as often as you can. Borrow or collect storytelling tapes or CDs. Join a story-sharing group where stories are told with simplicity and confidence. As you listen you will develop a discerning ear for stories, and for styles of telling.

You will hear stories that you like immediately, and some you don't, just as immediately. Later you will be able to analyze why that was so, and to weigh the teller's style and approach in the creation of the tale. Your own responses become the measure you will use to select your own material.

Read

No shortcut here. The search for a story is pleasant, but it takes time. Most storytellers will tell you that they read a dozen stories, or many more, before finding one to tell. I recommend beginning with traditional stories – myths, legends, folktales, fairy tales, fables – because they tell well and there is no richer source of wisdom and foible. Train your ears and eyes to pick out a good, tellable tale from the story confined on the printed page. Read the story aloud, for your eyes cannot always "hear" what it will sound like. The 398 section of your public library is the most generous, supportive, and accessible teacher one can find. Take your time. Read and dream. One of the joys of storytelling is that it suspends time in this frantic world.

Choose

Choosing a story is a little like a romance or a seduction. Or maybe love at first sight. As you thumb through collections of stories you may find yourself with opinions like "good, but not great" or "lame story." You begin the next one with mild interest, then a growing excitement. This story says, "You're mine!" This is the story that has plans for you.

The most common piece of advice is to tell stories that you love. Sounds reasonable and it is true, in part. Most of the stories you choose are the ones that you respond to almost immediately. Indeed, many tellers say they don't choose the stories, the stories choose them, which is a way of expressing the intense response that stories can excite. I tell my storytelling students to choose a story that they feel strongly about. Others have said choose one that touches you, or that you care about, or that means something to you. That leaves room for the story that you may not love exactly, but that you find arresting, or compelling. Here is the important thing: an emotional connection is essential if you are to tell the story the way it should be told. Your choices can be instructive. Ask yourself what appeals to you about that new story.

Evaluate

Get to know how stories work, because good stories have identifiable characteristics. Recognize those and you've gone a long way toward making good choices. Look at stories for structure, characters, cultural information, values, or teachings. Each story has a structure. The structure may vary depending upon the story type, but in the main, traditional tales depend upon a strong plot and a good deal of action. Characters move the plot along and provide the listener with someone to cheer for, and, perhaps, someone to vilify. Cultural information should accurately convey the culture from which the story comes. Values or teaching should be implicit in stories, not explicit, with the exception of fables. Look for the tale that conveys its wisdom by showing us, not telling us.

Grow

As you choose stories you may find yourself drawn to a particular sort of story. Tall tale, fable, ghost story: each has its charms and partisans. Although there are many generalists among storytellers, at least as many folks have an affinity for a story form and that's what they tell. You'll hear someone described as a tall tale teller, for instance. Pay attention to the forms that attract you and you may find yourself beginning to refine your choices.

When you move from a small, tightly held fistful of stories to a quite respectable story list, you might like to look at the variety of your selections. Do you find yourself attracted to stories that pose riddles? Are you inclined toward stories about romance? All very well, but be sure that your stories are varied and benefit from contrast.

This might be a good time to stretch. If you have never told a myth, it might be time to do so. Stories reveal their riches only in the telling, so try a new kind and see what happens.

Just as you will have identified the sorts of stories you tend to tell, so you may discover that stories from one culture consistently please you. We tend to rely on what is known, on what is familiar, and so our first choices often come from stories we already know.

Often those are stories from our own cultures. Borrowing stories from another culture carries with it the responsibility to learn enough about the culture to tell the tale knowledgeably. Scholarship and research are a part of becoming a storyteller. I like to remind my students that when we borrow an object of value from an acquaintance we try to treat it carefully and take very good care of it.

Choosing a story is not unlike choosing a garment. What items are on your list when you go shopping for a piece of clothing? Although we don't always practice it, we know one should buy only what one really prizes. Hard-earned cash deserves a purchase you're happy about. Your efforts as a storyteller should be spent on something important as well. You pay attention to fit, don't you? A garment has to look good, and feel good. That sinuous orange dress – remember? You knew enough about yourself to know what suited you and what didn't. You factor in the occasions you'll wear it also. Alteration is a fact of fashion life; sometimes you need a little hemming. Stories too are cut to fit. You choose one that suits and fits and is worth the effort. Then you begin to tell it and soon the story fits like a glove. ❧

Developing Your Story

by Caren Niele

The first rule of developing a story is that there is no right way to do it. There is only *your* way, the way that reflects your unique personality, perspective, and method of telling. The challenge is to determine the most effective approach for reaching your particular goal for each particular audience.

If we think of the development of a story in terms of the development of a child, we know that as humans grow, we pass through several predictable stages that add sophistication and mastery of skills. You will find that your relationship with a story will also grow from simple to complex.

Stage One: Getting to know the story

Have you ever seen toddlers "read" along with Mom or Dad when they've heard a story often enough? The first stage in developing the story is to experience it over and over. Because storytelling is an oral medium, you'll do well to read it into a tape recorder and listen to it as often as possible.

Be an active listener. While you're enjoying the story, think about what drew you to it. What message and atmosphere does it convey to you? Where does the story start? Do you recognize any patterns in the narrative? (Repetition was built into folktales in part to help out overworked storytellers. So take advantage of it!)

Stage Two: Learning the story sequence

The foundation of any story is plot. Professional storytellers have many techniques for setting the plot firmly in their minds. The best technique for you is the one that feels most comfortable. The only one that most storytellers discourage is memorization. When you memorize a story, you are locked into that version. You can't adapt it to your mood, or to your audience, which is a large part of the joy and power of storytelling. Equally important, if you experience the story through words rather than organically, through images, you transmit the sounds of words to your audience rather than those images. And what happens if you lose your place in the middle of telling? (Don't ask. It isn't pretty.)

Here are a few ways the pros learn their stories:

Outline – The same method that worked for you on those high school English papers will work here. After all, an outline is a logical, sequential flow of elements – just like a story.

Storyboard – You know how moviemakers get those exquisite images that speak volumes with a single shot? With storyboards. Storyboards are like comic strips; every picture carries on the plot from the preceding one. This is a great technique for the more visual-minded. And again, it helps you transmit images to your listeners.

Story mapping – Draw a flow chart or diagram of your story, starting at the "MIT" (see below) or at the beginning of the story.

MIT – Storytelling coach extraordinaire Doug Lipman developed a fascinating, if slightly more complex, approach to story-learning based on the "MIT" or "most important thing," the element in the story that drew you to tell it. Once you've determined your MIT – usually a central theme or episode – you can think of the story in terms of the events that lead up to and flow from it. Then you chart the events that lead to those events.

This is also the stage when you begin to tell the story to yourself without notes. When you feel confident, or ideally, even before you do, start telling to others. Nothing beats the feedback, direct and indirect, you gain from another person. As you progress through the later stages of story development, you will still benefit from telling the story to others. Think of it like riding a tandem bicycle. Sure, it's possible to ride alone. But it's not the same.

Throughout this process, and particularly at the beginning, you will want to return to the original text, or tape, to check that you have included all the essential details.

Stage Three: Getting over the humps with CAMELS

Once you know the plot of your story, six elements will help you bring it to life: Characters, Audience, Message, Energy, Language and Setting.

Characters – Good novelists write reams of "back story" to explain their characters' motivations, even if none of it makes its way into print. That's because every person, real or fictional, is the sum of his or her experiences.

What do your characters do in their spare time? What are their political views? You might wish to mentally place them in a situation totally different from that of the story, just to get to know them better.

One of the best ways to "get into" the physicality of a character is a well-known acting technique: Sit in a chair, feet flat on the floor, eyes closed. Listen to soothing music or meditate for a while, until you feel truly relaxed. Gradually begin to sit up, then stand, then walk, in character. The activity is not important; it's the attitude. Would your character hold his shoulders straight, or slouch? Walk fast or slowly? Ball her hands into fists?

Next, speak like the character. Choose any word – flower, potato, armchair – and repeat it over and over with your character's voice, inflection, rate of speech, tone, volume, etc.

Finally, put your character in a particular situation. (This works best with several people improvising at once.) How would your character open a stuck window? Return a defective item to a cashier? Get a seat on a crowded train? You do not have to use words for these improvisations; just nonsense syllables. If a character undergoes a dramatic transformation in the story – and the best ones usually do – you might repeat the entire exercise several times, based on her personality at different points in the story.

Audience – Are you preparing the story for fourth graders or for senior citizens? Do you have ten minutes to tell the story or just five? Most folk tales can be finetuned for almost any situation, with a little bit of work. You can add opportunities for audience participation (a plus for little ones especially), tone down violence, embellish descriptions, simplify language, add props (see below) – the possibilities are endless. The key is to get as much advance information about your audience as you can. I once went into a nursing home ready to tell stories about peace and tolerance, only to find that a murder had taken place there the previous week. My subject matter was good, but I had to think fast to rework some of the material.

Message – Do you like to be told the moral of a story? To me, it's like having a joke explained. If it isn't clear from the telling, forget it. Besides, a story may have several interpretations, depending on who is doing the telling and who is doing the listening. That said, we as tellers need to know what the story means to us, so we can shape every element to make our message as clear as possible. For example, depending on my interpretation of the Little Red Hen, I might emphasize the role of the overworked, under-appreciated Hen – by stressing her point of view through description, characterization, even where the story starts and ends – or I might choose to focus on the lazy farm animals instead.

Energy – Are you telling a rollicking tall tale or a Halloween chiller? One factor that determines the appropriate energy level for telling a story is the mood of the story itself. Another is your natural energy. And, since storytelling is a co-creation between teller and listener, the third factor is the energy level of your listeners. My energy level when telling tends to be on the high side. But when I go into a morning class of bleary-eyed high school students, I tone it down a bit, so as not to overwhelm them. When our energy is somewhat in sync with that of our audience, communication is a whole lot easier.

Language – Well-chosen words are the storyteller's stock-in-trade. Here is one instance when memorization can come in handy. First, it's a help to memorize your opening and closing lines, so you start and end the story on a strong note. Then, if you are telling a literary tale, if your tale requires repetition, ("I'll huff and I'll puff and I'll blow the house down!"), if you are speaking in an unfamiliar dialect, or if you have the good fortune to be able to create vivid, audience-appropriate word pictures, by all means memorize important words. And by the way, if you are using words from other cultures, be sure you know how to pronounce them!

Setting – Setting is such an important element of a story that it's been called a character in its own right. If you plan to tell stories from an unfamilar culture, I urge you to explore it. As with your characters, not everything you know about the culture will directly figure into your final product. But the authenticity of your work will skyrocket. Thanks to the Internet, this type of research is easier to do than ever.

Even if we tell a story from our own culture, we need to pay attention to setting. While we want to leave something to the imagination, the more our listeners have to work with – palm trees, glaciers, or heat so strong it melts unlit candles – the more completely they can enter the world of the story. Even just a few well-chosen images can do the trick.

Stage Four: Using your body and voice

Ernest Hemingway could rely only on his words when he wrote his stories. William Shakespeare had to trust his fellow actors. But you, as a storyteller, have total control over two elements of communication that are even more significant to your listeners than your words.

Communication scholars estimate that seventy-eight percent of what an audience retains from a speaker is visual. Fifteen percent is the sound, tone, volume, rhythm, etc. of the voice. And a mere seven percent of what an audience takes home is content! If that sounds far-fetched, consider this: If a student says she is very interested in what a teacher is saying, yet she says it sarcastically while looking out the window, what does the teacher believe?

Once you know your characters well, you will find that you usually don't need overly dramatic movements or vocal inflection to get them across to an audience. Every gesture, facial expression or intonation speaks volumes.

Stage Five: Using props, costumes, instruments

Can a story be told without props, costumes or instruments? Of course. And many of the best ones are. But these accoutrements come in handy, especially when working with young children.

Props can be as ornate as fancy puppetry or as simple as a fist "made up" with magic marker to resemble a face. Tellers for young children also use magnetic or flannel boards, which are perfect for manipulating characters. When using props, be sure they complement, but don't overpower your story. Also be sure that everyone in the audience can see them. Finally, be sure to rehearse with your props.

Costumes can add a wonderful visual dimension to your story, and they don't have to be expensive. Thrift shops and consignment stores are excellent sources. Again, rehearse in costume, so you know how it will feel, whether or not it restricts your movement, etc.

Finally, you don't have to be a musician to add musical accompaniment to your story. Traditional storytellers often had a drumbeat or other percussive element to keep the rhythm. Some tellers pick up a used ukulele or guitar and learn a few chords. Even a recorder, with the help of a couple of lessons or a book, will add extra texture, both to your stories and to the spaces between them.

Stage Six: Enjoy!

It's been said that a teller must perform a story up to twenty-five times to make it her own. Hopefully, this will be a labor of love rather than a life sentence! The joy of storytelling is in the personalization – making the story your own – and the reciprocality – the way teller and listener create the story experience together. Ideally, these are different with every telling.

In other words, we are always developing our stories, from the first telling to the last. ❧

Developing Personal Stories

by Barbara H. Clark

When telling stories from books, especially folktales, you work with a product that is already structured for you. When telling stories from life experiences, you must do the structuring yourself. To make a story "sing" requires inspiration, but it also requires story-shaping techniques. Personal stories, also called "life stories," should be carefully crafted if they are to have the same impact as stories from books.

Choosing a Subject

"I don't know what to write about, nothing interesting ever happens to me." "I've got so many things I want to write about, I don't know where to start." I've heard both of those comments from teens and adults in my storytelling workshops. Nonsense! Subjects for personal stories are already in your head, and deciding which one to use is simply a matter of selection.

Potential subjects generally fall into three broad categories: 1) a minor incident, 2) a memorable person, and 3) a major life-changing event. The minor incident may be as simple as a tooth extraction, a rainstorm, or a new pet. The memorable person may be a relative such as an ancestor or spouse; or it may be a mentor such as a teacher, or clergyman. The major life-changing event may be a marriage, earthquake, flood, birth, or death. You get the idea.

You might need to prime the pump of your memory by reviewing your life chronologically. Start with your childhood years: toys, pets, parents, siblings, grandparents. Move on to your school years: primary grades, junior high, high school, adolescent problems.

Consider early adulthood: college, work, courtship, marriage, childbirth. Examine your grown-up years: raising the family, new neighbors, home ownership, divorce, death, retirement.

Look at family photographs, old home movies or videos, and saved letters for ideas. Sit in a quiet place and think back on family stories, on your accomplishments, missed opportunities, embarrassments. Make a list of relationships and events that have shaped your life. Review, analyze, and rework the list continually.

The secret to a good story is not so much which subject you select, but what you do with it. Picking up a penny from the sidewalk can make a good story if properly structured.

Shaping the Story

Once you've settled on a subject, sit quietly and list ten things you want to say about it. Keep it simple. Start by writing brief vignettes. Include details like who, what, where, when, and how. Every story must have a beginning, middle and end. Why is that so important? Because if you don't know where you're going, you won't know when you get there. One of the most common defects of personal stories is the tendency to run on and on.

The beginning establishes the setting or goal for the story. The beginning settles your audience in their seats because they know where you're going. You must know up front what your story will deliver, then frame the beginning so that your audience is drawn into the world you will create. You're in Louisiana, not Alaska, which explains the gators; you want to buy jewelry for your spouse's birthday with only fifty bucks, that's why you're shopping in pawnshops. Get it?

The middle is the main body of the story. It develops the characters, establishes your point of view, and dramatizes incidents. Use description. Create a scene that the audience will "see, hear, and even smell." Rather than saying, "She wore a pretty dress," describe the dress so the audience will "see" how pretty it is. Use dialogue. The people in your story should talk. Convey their attitudes and personalities through conversation. Don't say, "He was angry." Give him dialogue and behavior that convey anger. Portray the people in your stories as you see them, for they are your characters. Make them real; give them life. The middle also leads gradually to the crisis point or climax, and every story should have one. The climax needn't be world-shattering, it might be quiet and introspective, and it may be located either in the middle itself or in a surprise ending.

The ending is usually the most difficult to write. It must provide a solution to the problem or crisis posed in the story, or bring closure to the series of events described. The ending may be a slap-dang zinger, or a calm "ah-h-h-h," but either way, it should leave the audience with a sense of completeness. Above all, it must make sense. If not, explain why. It should also tell the audience how you were affected by the events in the story. What did you learn? How were you changed? After all, it is your story. Finally, your story should have a point. If you haven't decided what the point of your story is, how can the listener discover it? If you don't have a point, you don't really have a story.

Fine Tuning

When you think you've finished creating your story, write it down. When you think you've finished writing your story, you haven't. Go back and start all over again. Like the man said, "There's no such thing as good writing, only good rewriting." You must rework, delete, add, shift, correct, etc., all the things needed to "fine tune" a story. Pare it down to the bare essentials, and trim out all unnecessary words. Don't be afraid to add humor and irony. While your aim might simply be to entertain, try also to be inspiring, provocative, or maybe even educational. Give your audience something to think about later.

Just writing down the facts doesn't tell the full story. You must give the story "soul." And remember, it's a personal story, so put yourself into the story. Don't be deterred by other people's accounts of how something happened. If your sister doesn't agree with your version of events, tell her to create her own story!

When you're ready to test your story on a live audience, remember all of your public speaking techniques: voice control, body language, gestures, eye contact, etc. Tell the story as though you were having a conversation with a friend. If you enjoy sharing your story, the audience will enjoy listening to it.

Personal stories can be wonderful when done well. Do your homework. Be wonderful! ❧

Taking Care of the Audience

by Glenn Morrow

Storytelling is powerful. It deeply affects our emotions, memories, and imagination. You have no doubt felt this power when listening to a skillful storyteller. Listening to a story is like being taken on a journey. Each listener's journey is different, but each listener relies on the storyteller to be a trustworthy guide. Being trustworthy means being responsive to and taking care of the audience.

When we engage a mountain guide, we want to know three basic things: Does the guide know the way? Is the guide in shape to complete the journey? Do we trust the guide to lead us safely home? The same basic questions apply to the storyteller as guide to the imagination.

Knowing the way in story goes beyond knowing the story. A guide should know how long the journey will take. Time your telling. When you first start performing, shorter is better. As a general rule, telling a story takes longer than reading it aloud. Many stories that deeply engage listeners in a timeless sense of listening are only a single page in length. In different contexts and different cultures stories may vary enormously in length, but as a general rule a story that clocks in at less than ten minutes will probably work for any audience except very young children. (They need very short stories with a lot of audience interaction or visuals to hold their attention). If you find your story text is more than a handful of pages in length, or your telling takes significantly longer than ten minutes, you should seriously consider the context in which you are telling. Is a long story appropriate for that setting? For that audience? Look at where you can prune your story, or how you can make it into several different and shorter stories or episodes.

Being in shape to guide the journey means that the audience never has to take care of you. If your emotions are interfering with your ability to tell the tale, you are not yet ready to tell it to strangers. Sometimes we are surprised by how deeply telling a story can affect us, even when we can speak the facts of the story quite calmly. This obviously applies to personal stories, but occasionally a folktale or fairy tale may affect us just as deeply. Work with trusted friends until you can tell the tale without choking up or bursting into tears. When you tell a story, any story, you expose a part of your self. Sometimes that is harder than we expect. Don't attempt to take a short cut by telling something that happened to you as if it happened to someone else, as in "This happened to a friend of mine…" That usually doesn't work. You will find it hard to maintain the third person perspective, and your audience will very likely not be fooled. Once listeners think you are trying to deceive them, you've lost them.

A good guide is confident. It is always a mistake to begin a performance by apologizing for a story or for performance skills. Don't worry if you forget a detail. You can usually slip it in later by saying something like, "What you need to know is…" Your audience wants you to succeed. Acknowledge that support by telling with confidence.

A trusted story guide looks out for the safety of the audience – all of the audience. The power of story is that it takes a unique shape in the mind of each listener. Observe your audience as you tell. Some listeners may have strong reactions to a story. Storytellers are not therapists (though many therapists use storytelling as part of their work). Therapy is not your job. But you don't want to take listeners to a place in memory or imagination and strand them there. If your tale is going to a dark and snaky place, think carefully about how you are going to get home. Older children love scary stories, but these same stories can cause nightmares for their younger brothers and sisters. A story that is fine at a potluck may not be so fine when told in a hospital ward. A personal story about a life trauma can echo a similar event that happened to a listener. Imagine yourself hearing the story just after that trauma occurred. Did the storyteller create the safety you needed? Did the storyteller clue you in to where the story was going, or were you ambushed by the story? Did the story bring you back into the light?

Traditional tales typically build in safety for the listener. They begin "Long ago and far away" (not here, not now). They typically end with some form of justice. If you find this justice harsh, pick another story. Don't change the ending. If the story slays the monster (dragon, wolf, witch, troll) at the end, then the monster is dead. If you change that ending, then the monster is still lurking out there in your listener's imagination. Young listeners especially need clear-cut justice at the end of the tale: the good rewarded, the wicked punished.

A well-told story is a wonderful journey for your audience. It may simply amuse, or it may tell a hard truth, but if the teller thinks about his or her responsibilities as a guide, the story will always feel like a gift. For that is what a story is: a gift. ❦

Where to Get Started

by Katy Rydell

Be gentle with yourself. When you're ready to tell your first story in public, find a good, safe place. When I started out, I had the good fortune to hear about a local group of adults who get together once a month to tell stories. In those days, I was so shy I could barely open my mouth. For six months I went to Community Storytellers meetings and never spoke a word to anyone, onstage or off. Eventually I realized that it wasn't right to absorb all that wonderful energy without giving anything back, so I got up my nerve to tell a story. It was a great place to begin. A supportive audience, experienced listeners, laughter, applause. Wow. I loved it.

At Community Storytellers, I had more good fortune, and that was to hear the advice of experienced tellers. One said, "Never underestimate the work you do for free." Another said, "Get yourself a laboratory where you can practice stories." Following their advice, I volunteered to tell stories at a local child guidance clinic. Once a week for six months, I went to the clinic and told stories to children after school. My audience was small and sweet. They listened. I grew. After six months I had a huge repertoire of stories, many of which I haven't told since. I had learned which stories fit me, and which didn't. I had learned how to learn a story, how to plan a program, how to interact with an audience. It was a great experience.

Len Cabral says, "Volunteer in as many places as you can find. Every experience will hold a lesson." He's right.

Day Care Centers

Len got started back in the early seventies when he had a job as a teacher's assistant in a day care center. Before lunch it was his job to settle the children down by reading them a story. He was in charge of between ten and fifteen five-year-olds, all of them tired, cranky, rambunctious, and hungry. When Len's eyes were on the book, the children were often pinching and pushing each other. When he stopped reading to settle them down, the story stopped; when he started reading again, the children started wiggling again. They also complained, aloud: "I can't see the pictures." "Show me again." "You're moving the book too fast."

Len soon realized that the only way he could tell a story and keep track of the children at the same time was to put the book down and tell the story. So he did. "Once there was a rabbit who had big floppy ears and a long bushy tail. His name was Gilbert." Len paused. Gilbert, one of the most active boys in the class, stopped in mid-pinch. His face lit up and he yelled, "Shhh! It's about me! Listen!" As the story continued, Len included the names of other children. One by one, they stopped and stared in amazement. Hands stopped poking. Fingers stopped pinching. Instead of complaints and bickering, Len saw big eyes and smiling faces. He writes, "I saw the faces of children engaged. I knew I had discovered something very valuable. I had discovered the value of storytelling in the classroom." The children made a discovery too: that they could have a better time if they could listen longer. Over time, Len watched their attention spans grow from two minutes to three, four, and five minutes.

Sometimes he asked the children if they would like to act a story out. Yes, they would. Then they had an even stronger motivation for listening attentively. The fun of creative dramatics was a welcome reward for their developing listening skills.

Classrooms

Maybe you know a teacher. Maybe you know a student. Volunteer to tell in a classroom. Even if your ultimate goal is to tell for adults, you'll gain valuable experience. The skills you acquire telling in front of one audience will help you with the next.

Libraries

Gay Ducey started by taking a class in storytelling in the University of California Berkeley Library School. She remembers being "amused that there was a class doing what my family had done for generations." Later, someone who had been in the class asked Gay to come and tell a story at the library. She did. A month or two later, she was invited to tell again. Occasionally other people called up and asked her to come to their libraries.

Every now and then over the next year, someone called with yet another request for a story. By the end of a year, Gay had a career as a storyteller.

Talk to your local librarian about storytelling opportunities.

What If I Don't Want to Tell Stories to Children?

Not all storytellers start out by telling to children. There are many places where you can tell stories to adults. You know what your life is like. Take a look at it from a storyteller's perspective. What organizations do you belong to, what meetings do you attend, what committees do you serve on? Is there a service organization in your life? A religious organization? Offer to tell a story at the next meeting.

Take a look at your social life, too. Is there a retirement party coming up? A wedding? An opening of an art exhibit? A story can be a lively contribution to a social event.

Are you taking a class in any of the language arts – poetry, fiction, stand-up comedy, autobiography? Offer to tell a story. Fellow students who are unfamiliar with storytelling will be exposed to this art form, and you will get more experience.

Senior Centers

If you're looking for adult audiences, you're guaranteed to find them at senior centers. Barbara Clark has performed extensively for seniors and has a few suggestions on how to make a performance work well. If you're telling at a day-care site, plan your program immediately before lunch. Seniors who are dropped off for the day will have arrived, and they'll be alert and responsive. After lunch some might be lethargic and doze off.

If you're telling at a recreation center site, schedule your program immediately following a meeting, but before the refreshment break. Most people won't leave before they've had refreshments.

Do People Tell Stories at Work?

Peggy Prentice, one of the co-founders of Community Storytellers in Southern California, was a secretary in the aerospace industry. One Halloween, at lunch hour, her colleagues received brown paper bags with peanut butter sandwiches, an apple, and candy pumpkins. Peggy led them in a raucous rendition of a children's participation story, *Let's Go On a Witch Hunt*. Peggy's colleagues, accustomed to seeing her as a demure and dignified corporate secretary, were amazed at how animated she was. That program, she said, was one of the most successful programs she ever gave.

Peggy told stories in the place where she worked, but not as part of her job. There are many people, however, whose stories are very much part of their professional lives.

Peter Rydell was a researcher for RAND, also in Southern California. He once opened a presentation for senior military personnel with the words, "Once upon a time." Heads whipped around. Peter then launched into a traditional folktale, one that summarized the overall message of his speech. He said that telling a story at a RAND briefing felt like cheating, because it made his job so much easier. It was easier to get people's attention, to get them relaxed, and to make points effectively.

Other Places to Start

Try your friends. Your family.

Find a group of storytellers near you.

Take a storytelling class or workshop.

Attend the annual NSN conference held each summer. The conferences are full of workshops, ideas, and lots of other storytellers who can give you even more ideas.

Local groups, classes, workshops, conferences: NSN can help you find those. Look in *Storytelling Magazine,* look on the website, or contact your local State Liaison. NSN is a community of people who care about storytelling at all levels, in all situations. Let us help.

Don't Forget to Listen

Attend storytelling groups, attend performances, go to festivals. Hear as many stories as you can, from as many different storytellers as you can. You'll increase your vocabulary, not just your story vocabulary, but also your style of telling vocabulary.

Are There Bad Places to Start?

Yes. Talk to other performers. We all have horror stories to tell.

Peggy Prentice once tried to tell stories at a senior center, at noon, at a time when the seniors normally played bridge. They showed up with their lunches, expecting to play cards, and were irritated when they couldn't. They opened their lunch bags, rattling the paper noisily, and ate and talked while Peggy tried to tell stories. Nobody had a good time.

Don't try to tell stories at the finish line of a 10K race. Peggy tried that, too.

Peggy got into trouble at the bridge-playing senior center and at the 10K race not only because she was a beginner, but because the event organizers were beginners too. They didn't know what storytelling was. They didn't understand that listeners need to be prepared to listen, and they need to be able to hear. If someone invites you to tell a story in an unfamiliar situation, try to find out if they know what they're asking for.

Be wary of telling stories anywhere outdoors. Acoustics are often poor. Loud music or a neighbor with a chain saw can overwhelm your voice and your audience's attention.

Some people recommend hospitals as good places to start storytelling. I don't. I think hospitals are difficult, challenging storytelling environments, fraught with peril. People go to hospitals because they are sick. Children are lonely, scared, and bewildered. Save hospital telling until after you have more experience.

When Should I Start Charging for Performances?

In the beginning, the places you volunteer have more to offer you than you have to offer them. They offer you experience performing before a real, live, wiggling, coughing, reacting audience. That experience is invaluable.

Later, after you have a repertoire and experience, after you know which style and which stories fit you as a storyteller, and which stories fit different audiences, then you can think about charging. Talk to storytellers in your area to get an idea of the going rate. That rate will vary from community to community, and from venue to venue. How long is the program? How big is the audience? How far do you have to travel? Many factors affect how much you should charge. You'll probably want to start at the lower end of the spectrum while you build your resume.

Remember that your relationship with copyright law changes once you begin charging for performances. If you are a librarian or a teacher, the law protects your right to tell a copyrighted story in an educational situation; the law does not protect your right to tell it as a freelance performer.

When should you start charging for your stories? Donald Davis has a good answer: "When they want to pay you. You'll know."

Don't be in a hurry to "go professional." Let storytelling always be, first and foremost, a joy. ❧

Len Cabral's comments are adapted from *Len Cabral's Storytelling Book* by Len Cabral and Mia Manduca. Neal-Schuman Publishers. 1997

Barbara Clark's comments are adapted from "Telling Stories to Seniors," published in *STORIES*, Spring 2000.

After Telling – Evaluation

by Margaret Read MacDonald

One of the most important steps you will take in your storytelling career is evaluation. Evaluating your own performance, finding a trusted other to provide feedback, keeping a storytelling journal – these are important steps. Don't skimp on your time here.

Keep a Journal

After each telling write yourself a brief note remembering the audience and their responses. Note the tales you told and their fit or mis-fit for this audience. Make notes about anything that went poorly and suggestions for avoiding this in future.

Most important of all, note things which went really well! Try to understand how you achieved this success. In the heat of the telling moment you will suddenly create an unplanned moment of brilliance. Be sure to note this down, or you may never do it again!

Find a Critique Partner

Build a relationship with a critique partner. This should be someone who understands your aesthetic values and your telling aims. Place this person in your audience now and then to assess your work. Only a close personal contact such as this will be apt to give you the serious, hard-to-swallow critiquing you need to hear. You must, in turn, critique your partner's work.

Consult a Checklist

I provide a checklist to my students for self-critiquing right after their performances. Here are the points I suggest they consider:

Value of Performance

- What was the value of this performance to you?
- What was the value of this performance to the separate audience members?
- What was the value of this performance to the group as a whole?

Communication and Audience Caretaking

- Did you really *see* your audience?
- Were you trying to communicate with them as you told?
- Were you taking care of the audience and aware of their needs and responses?

These are perhaps the most important questions you should be asking yourself. You are there to serve your audience. Their needs are paramount. If at any moment you are thinking about yourself, rather than about your audience, you are dropping the ball.

Delivery

- Did you take time to pause and collect yourself and your audience before you launched into your tale?
- Did you use your voice well to carry your tale's meanings?
- Did your body tell the tale with you? If not, how can you help your body join your voice, mind, and heart in communicating with your audience?
- Was your ending skillful? Effective?
- Did you allow your listeners to savor the ending in their own ways before breaking the story trance?

Scripting

- Did the script communicate the tale's meanings well?
- Did the language flow easily?

- Was the language you spoke as fine as you had intended?
- Mark the text for spots you need to work on.

Control

- Were you in complete control of your story?
- Did you know what you wanted to communicate well enough to relax and enjoy the sharing?

Plan for the Next Telling

To be able to answer yes to those questions you need only one thing: experience! Where can you tell this story again?

Of all the suggestions above, the most important is the last. To become good at your art you must tell again and again and again. Don't wait for storytelling opportunities to come to you. Go out and drum them up. And keep critiquing. No two performances are alike. One day you are perfect, the next not so hot. Keep telling and keep critiquing to get it better *most* of the time!

Tape It

Make a tape recording of your performance. This can be done easily by sticking a tape recorder under your chair or laying it on a table beside you. The quality is not so important. You just need a record of what you are doing. This can be used for self-critiquing, but unless you videotape, you are getting only a fraction of the telling event – the voice. However, the audiotape serves an important function in providing a record of your own tale text for future reference. To self-critique your gestures, you can ask a friend to videotape you. But again this is only a part of the event. It is the combination of teller and audience that is the heart of things. ✿

Don't Stand Under the Clock: Performance Tips

by Nancy Schimmel

What do I do about nervousness?

In performing, I find a little nervousness is not a bad thing. It keeps me on my toes, alert to the audience and listening to the story, so I don't lose my place. The trick is to not show your nervousness. The problem is that you don't always know how you show it. I didn't know until I saw a video of myself. I lick my lips. A video (or your best friend) can tell you what you do: wring your hands, say "uh" at the beginning of each phrase, clear your throat (bad for your voice!), brush your hair out of your eyes. Once you are aware of your habit, you can work on breaking it (or get a haircut). Here's a tip from my voice teacher: if nervousness makes your mouth dry, clenching your teeth a couple of times or biting your tongue may fool your salivary glands into thinking you are eating and they will start to work again. Also remember to breathe: stage fright is excitement without breathing.

How do I arrange a full program?

I like to start a program with a short story so listeners new to storytelling will get a quick pay-off and an idea of what an oral story is like. Then I might tell a longer story, perhaps one that requires more concentration from the listener. Then I change the pace with a song or a story that encourages audience movement, and end with a story that is an attention-keeper, either through suspense, humor, or audience participation. This is not a rule, and the pattern will certainly need to be varied at times. If the attention-keeper has a violent ending or sad theme, I would probably follow it with something upbeat or comforting.

Starting with a short story may be enough to give the audience an idea of what's coming up. Sometimes I'll want to let them know more. I may tell them I'll be asking them to participate. That way, if their teacher has just ordered complete silence, they will know there are exceptions (and so will the teacher). I also try to remember to let the audience know when I'm about to tell the last story, so they are not caught by surprise by the program's ending. If I will be selling books and recordings afterwards, I mention that just before the last story, so the program ends with a story, not with a sales pitch.

I like to have a theme for a program, though it's not necessary. A theme helps me go from one story to the next in a simple, conversational way, and helps me remember which one I'm doing next. (I usually have a large-print set list at my feet as well.) A story or song that doesn't fit the theme at first glance may fit well if I point out the connection when I introduce it. This can give me a fresh approach to the story. A theme can also send me off to find new material.

How should I introduce my stories?

I usually don't announce the title of a story before I tell it, especially if the title gives away something better disclosed during the course of the story. And I almost never say: "Here is a story about…" because the same story can be about different things to different people. I'd rather say, "Here is a story from West Africa" or "This is a story I learned from my mother."

Sometimes I want to tell a story that I have issues with. For example, I tell one story in which the women do all the cooking. I introduce that story by saying, "In this story we go to a time long ago before daddies knew how to make supper; or at least they claimed they didn't know how, so they didn't have to do it. So they never understood that when someone has gotten supper together, they want you there to eat it while it's hot. Well, this particular daddy, who was a farmer, started off to the corner store way late in the afternoon, never thinking how close to suppertime it was…"

If I'm telling a story about a bad stepmother, I'll follow it with a story about a good stepmother, and when I'm telling the story about a bad stepmother, I use my introduction to make it clear that her wickedness is an exception, not a rule.

It was my audience that had issues with one story I told. When a bearchild killed a seal, my Marin County fourth-to-sixth-grade audience gasped. After that, I started introducing the story by explaining why hunting was vital to the survival of the Inuit people.

I usually warn the audience if I am going to tell a scary or bloody story; then they can brace themselves, and say "That wasn't so scary" afterwards.

If you want the audience to help with the story (and you always do, if only by paying attention) the introduction is a vital element. You might introduce Esphyr Slobodkina's *Caps for Sale* by saying: "This story has monkeys in it. Now monkeys are supposed to copy what someone else does. So when I do this [shake a finger] you do this (shake a finger and say "tss tss tss"). With older children, who are more self-conscious about joining in, I don't usually say anything in advance, just smile and nod when a few join in a repeated part.

Be careful about asking your audience questions in a story unless you are prepared to deal with the unexpected answer.

What do I need to know about the performance setting?

Stories can be told almost anywhere, under almost any circumstances, though I have found that doing a story program in competition with a nearby bagpiper is a losing proposition. At a shopping mall, fair, or other outdoor setting, it is good to have a friend or assistant to steer wandering musicians or loud conversations elsewhere. Another storyteller, who can protect you and spell you, is even more useful, as it is usually easier to keep a crowd than to attract one in a situation where other events are competing with the storytelling. Stories with some visual element such as paperfolding or string tricks, large gestures, or musical instruments can serve to attract an audience. People setting up a big outdoors event with a small space for storytelling always tell you that you will be far enough away from the main stage that the rock band won't bother you. They are always wrong. Always. Don't plan to tell any complicated, tender, poetic or creepy stories there. This is the time for lively, funny, short or repetitive stories.

Ideally, I like to tell in a fairly quiet but not silent place. I like a barrier behind me so the audience is not distracted by passers-by, but no barrier defining the limits of the audience area, so people feel free to come and go, and to listen while pretending not to. Circumstances, of course, are rarely ideal. I try to think ahead to avert interruptions – can we disconnect the intercom announcement system? Have the person introducing us ask people to turn off all cell phones and other personal electronic devices? But the best insurance is to know the story well enough to be able to stop, wait for the fire engines to go by, and pick up the thread again without getting lost.

How should I handle interruptions?

There are several ways to handle interruptions from young audience members in school or library programs. Some of them can be prevented by saying, "If you know this story, just smile, and I'll know you know it, but let's keep the ending a secret between us." If the interruption is a question related to the story that can be answered briefly, I do so. Other questions and comments I try to acknowledge but not answer. It's no use trying to ignore them; the child will just think you didn't hear and will repeat the comment more loudly. Nod, or say "That's nice," or "I'll tell you later," and go on. Then pick up on it when the story is over. Another adult should be present to take care of needs that can't wait.

It's tempting to pay more attention to the most interested listeners, and this does give you good energy for telling, but with young audiences, it's prudent to make eye contact with the restless ones as well, as this may help them focus. If you are telling for the first time, and are convinced that looking people in the eye will make you forget the entire story, look just over their heads.

What other details do I need to think about?

Workshop rooms are often set up with straight rows of chairs. I like to curve the ends of each row forward. This makes the room feel more like a storytelling space with not much effort. If nobody sits in the first row of chairs, I take them away, and the populated second row becomes the first row. In classrooms I prefer not to be placed under the clock if I can help it, or in front of windows. I'd rather have the sun in my eyes than in the audience's. I want them to see the expression on my face but I can manage without clearly seeing the expressions on theirs. In an auditorium, I like soft light on the audience, because storytelling is a collaboration between them and me, and if it is completely dark out there I find myself futilely straining to see their faces.

Before you set out for the performance space, think about what you will need. A bottle of water? A quiet spot in which to collect yourself before you go on? A small table to put props on? A chair that doesn't squeak? Directions (to the place, and then to the bathroom)? A phone number to call in case you get lost or delayed? Someone to help you bring in your equipment? A microphone that is NOT attached to a lectern? A microphone stand? As I plan a program, I make two lists (sometimes on the same piece of paper): What I am going to tell, and what I need to bring or ask for.

What do I do if I make a mistake?

To present a successful program, you do not have to tell each story perfectly. Recordings (where corrections can be made electronically) give us a false standard of perfection. Live performance, however, has an excitement that more than makes up for small lapses of memory. The audience wants you to succeed. If you realize you have forgotten to say something early in the story that the audience needs to know now, just slide it in. As you gain experience, you will learn to cope with your mistakes without cringing or apologizing. When a teller I know forgot to have Jack put the grains of corn in his pocket before he set out on his journey, she had him use seeds from the pumpkins in the witch's house instead. Now she always tells it that way. This is how the folk process works, and you are now part of it! ❧

This article was adapted from Nancy Schimmel's book, *Just Enough to Make a Story: A Sourcebook for Storytelling*, now in its third edition. Sisters' Choice Press. 1992.

Dealing with Stage Fright

by Elizabeth Ellis

When the subject of fear is mentioned among story-tellers, stage fright is usually the first thing we think of. People often say to me, "Oh, I know you don't ever have to deal with stage fright, because you have been telling stories for years." I always laugh whenever I hear someone say that! Having a lot of experience may make some situations easier to deal with, but I do not think stage fright ever really goes away. Put in a new or demanding situation, any teller can fall victim to it.

All of us are familiar with the symptoms: sweaty palms, shortness of breath, feeling cold and clammy or downright nauseous. (Yes, I have been so frightened, I have thrown up at festivals. I am grateful it has not happened lately, but I am not cocky enough to think that it can never happen again.)

Current advice about the jitters usually includes imagining the people in the front row in their underwear. I guess that is supposed to help us relax. My imagination, however, is so vivid I find the idea distracting, even provocative if the right people are present.

What can you do when you are overcome with stage fright?

I really do have a suggestion, but first I want to make the point that the best time to deal with stage fright is long before it happens. Knowledge is often the antidote. The better you know your story the less you have to be nervous about. So, make sure you give yourself ample time to prepare. The more important the event is, the more time you may need in order to feel prepared. "Feeling prepared" can take more time than actually "being prepared." That's why the opportunity to share your story with small groups of supportive people before the event is so useful.

Knowledge about your listeners is important, too. Please don't assume. Instead, ask lots of questions. The better you know your audience ahead of time, the more effective your planning for the event will be. Careful planning increases the confidence you can feel that you have chosen stories your audience will enjoy hearing.

Gather information about the event, as well. How much time do you have? What part do you play in the overall program? Will there be other storytellers? What other things will the participants have experienced before they hear you tell? If possible, speak to another teller who has told at this event in the past. If that is not an option, talking to someone who has been part of an event of this type can be helpful. Most tellers are happy to share their successes with others. Some will even speak honestly about their failures, bless their hearts.

Knowledge helps build confidence. However, you can be well prepared and still experience a bout of white-knuckled terror. What then? Breathe. Yep, it's that simple. Breathe. Fear is excitement without any breath. When we get frightened, we begin to restrict our breathing. We begin to breathe ragged, shallow breaths from the back of our throat. That actually increases our experience of fear. Stop and breathe. Focus on your breathing. Breathe in as deeply as you can. Breathe from your solar plexus. Try to fill your entire being.

Enthusiasm can be thought of as the opposite of fear. The term comes from two Greek words, *en* and *theos*. Its original meaning was to be "filled with the breath of God." So breathe. Fill yourself with the breath of the Divine, whatever that means for you. Being filled with the breath of the Divine leaves no room for fear. Stage fright will dissolve naturally, leaving you with calmness and confidence.

Thoreau told us, "The only way out is through." Do not let stage fright keep you silent. Every teller has experienced it. None of them ever died from it! Acknowledge your feelings and move forward. Trust your stories. Trust your listeners. Most of all, trust yourself. You are up to the challenge of growing as a teller. So go out there and tell. Just don't forget to breathe. ❧

Taming the Wild Beast: Family Audiences and Survival

by Bill Harley

About sixteen years ago, I made the decision to focus more of my work on family audiences. The switch was not easy. Working with broad age spans requires a flexibility and ability to work on several different levels, which is challenging even for seasoned performers. Some of my early shows were nightmares. Some still are. It took me a long time to develop a sense of balance – to learn how to speak to adults while still honoring children, and vice versa. It took me a long time to learn what I needed to ask for in order for the show to be a good one. I'm still learning.

The rewards for working with multi-age groups are large. As a performer, one of my central goals through my entire career has been to build community. A community usually involves someone who is different from you. A multi-age audience fits the bill.

Everyone there has different needs. The ten-year-old needs something of relevance. So does the four-year-old. So does the forty-year-old. But they're all in different places. The four-year-old needs some physical activity and repetition. The ten-year-old needs some goofiness, and thumbing of nose at authority. The forty-year-old needs some thoughtfulness, and knowledge that their four- and ten-year-old are enjoying the experience. The four- and ten-year-old desperately want their parent to like the thing they like. They all need to be reminded of things they hold in common. When I can bring all these elements to my performance, the group as a whole shares something, and leaves not quite the same.

Here are some things I've learned (and relearned) about multi-age shows:

Environment

There is nothing more important than making sure that the performance environment is conducive to your work. You have to demand certain things.

- The audience has to be able to hear you. If you don't have your own portable system, you should get one. Keep it in your car – it will save your life. Or get very good at telling people exactly what you need. If they are having trouble getting the sound to work, be willing to wait until they have it figured out. They will not remember that the sound system didn't work – they will remember that you couldn't hold the audience.

- The audience should be able to see you. This requires that the sight lines are okay – make sure people in the back can see you. If it is a big place, you need to have some lights on you. Generally, it helps if the lights are brighter where you are than where everyone else is. I don't have a hard and fast rule about lighting the audience. Sometimes it seems to work, sometimes I think it's better off dark. Having the house dimmed at least a little tends to cut down on the distraction of movement in the audience, which will happen when there are very young kids.

  Carry with you the idea that the performance space is your home – a place the audience is being welcomed into. There should be a feeling of specialness about the space. When lights are down and the stage is lit, it adds to the excitement for kids. It still works for me.

- Don't let there be too large a physical space between you and the audience. There is an inverse, exponential relationship between the distance between you and the first row of people and how easy it is to get your audience involved. If you perform in one of those dumb high school auditoriums that has forty yards between you and the first permanent row of seats, get them to put folding chairs in between. Which leads to:

- Do not, do not, do not allow four-year-olds to sit at your feet and forty-year-olds to sit in the back. That is a cute idea, and cute ideas are almost always very stupid. Is this a family show? Then have the families sit together. Let the parents be the disciplinarians, and let families enjoy each other's company during the show. I almost always refuse to perform if there are sixty kids in the front and a bunch of parents in the back. It is the single most common reason for a bad show. You may copy this page and bring it with you to show the sponsor. I give my permission – not that I count for all that much.

- Get rid of distractions – listen when you go into the space. Is there a blower on? Get the custodian to turn it off. Is there a spotlight focused far stage left? Get them to turn it off. Did they set you up next to the Balboni Family Fireworks display at the outdoor festival? Or Santa? Tell them you need a quieter place or you can't work.

- Ask that someone else be in charge of monitoring the hall. Sometimes you have to address outrageous behavior, but it's better to put someone else in charge of being the bad cop and impress upon them how important their job is.

As far as environment goes, there are two things to keep in mind: a) Tell them early what you need, when you first talk. Send a list. When you get there, it's usually too late, and b) arrive early so you can do some damage control.

Remember "But we've always done it this way" is not a reasonable answer. Changing the environment changes the rules, and you will be more in charge. We should change the rules all the time.

Material

Finding the right material for a family audience is hard. Even when you find the material, it can take dozens of times performing it to learn how to use it so it reaches everyone. Here are some rules of thumb to keep in mind.

- Pay attention to each age group. All ages will tolerate something not aimed at them if they know that someone else is truly being entertained and the performer is going to get back to them eventually. I don't mind taking a digression in a story to aim a joke at the adults as long as it's not too long, and it's not patronizing or dishonoring children. Kids will wait while you direct a line to adults; adults will wait while you do something completely silly. And remember kids learn through context and inference more than they do through direct instruction – if you use "abomination" in a story more than once, the kids will figure it out, or ask the parent next to them (if you've insisted the parent be there). Kids love the word "abomination."

- Vary content and style. I am committed to using music in my performance because I think people use a different part of their brain with music than with spoken story. Music is one option, but there are many ways to tell a story. Whether it's a string story, or something in verse, or a participation story, it helps to mix approaches. Of course, this is just good advice generally, but it's especially true for family audiences.

- Be aware of the lowest common denominator. I suspect that most ships in the family performance world are wrecked upon the rocks of three- and four-year-olds. They always come, because it's not fair to leave them at home with a baby-sitter and bring just the ten-year-old. They will determine how long the show goes. If they are not served, by giving them a simple line that they can repeat, or a story that is very closely related to their lives, or a physical action they can do, they will be in the aisles, not paying attention to you. Arrrrrrgh! It's the way it works, and this is where you can get into trouble by not being flexible. You can go out on the sea of story for four or five minutes at a time, but you have to come back and give them something, or you'll be sorry. If you hate that, family audiences aren't for you. This is not true if the audience goes to about seventy percent or more adult – then all the rules change – but it is true for anything below it. Find out how to add material for the older kids and adults to the songs and stories that are especially aimed at young ones. The real story of the five little ducks! Repetition for the little ones, sibling rivalry and fratricide for the nine-year-olds, and the ironical view of the duck mother for the adults.

The Art of Performing

In addition to material and environment, there is the actual art of performing – establishing a relationship with the audience. Developing that relationship is an art form, and it requires relaxation and presence.

- Learn to put up with a little white noise. There will be some kids in the aisle. Some baby will cry out. Some wise guy nine-year-old will make a comment when it's quiet. Roll with the punches. Stay focused in your performance. And learn to decide when those distractions have become part of the performance. When the four-year-olds are charging the stage, or the baby is still crying after five minutes, that's when you have to address them. You can do it honestly and openly if you're direct, lighthearted, and kind.

One of my favorite stories about performance is being hit twice by two nine-year-olds with spitballs in front of five hundred people. Nobody else noticed. They loaded up a third time. I tried to shake my head at them, but they paid no attention. I was very tired, and didn't want to be hit again. I stopped mid-sentence and said, "Don't you dare shoot those spitballs." The audience gasped, the culprits gagged, and I went right back into the story like nothing had happened. It was great. I bet they still remember it.

Usually, something a little less direct suffices. ("Suddenly, the king heard a baby cry in the distance…")

- Know when to get off. More is not better, even when it feels like it. I aim for an hour. Sometimes I quit right then – if things are going well, I might go an extra ten minutes. Leave them wanting more. This is very important. Less is okay, as long as you're clear with the presenter about what they can expect. At the forty-minute point in the show, I begin the race for the curtain and tend to incorporate more pieces that require participation. I try to end up with everyone doing something together.

It has taken me a long time to relax and enjoy family audiences. Like the girl in the rhyme, when they're good they're very, very good and when they're bad they're horrid. But after a while, comfort will come. The rewards are very large – at times it feels like "This is the way it's supposed to be, everyone together." It's good work. It needs to be done. ✯

Excerpted from a longer article published in *The Museletter*, February 1997.

Caring for Your Instrument: The Voice

by Bonnie Greenberg

Your voice is part of a larger system – your whole body – that requires careful maintenance to perform at its best. Remember: your voice is your instrument. The more you care for it, the better it will sound. Think of yourself as being in training. Like most athletes, you want to keep yourself tuned up for peak performance.

Your Body

The body responds well to getting plenty of rest, good nourishment, lots of water (eight glasses a day if possible), and proper attire (neck scarves and earmuffs in cold climates in winter).

Exercise regularly to improve breath control and overall body tone.

Learn relaxation exercises so that you can use them for warm-ups and general stress reduction at any time. Invest in a good relaxation tape.

Eat nourishing foods. On performance days, don't drink whole milk or eat dairy products as they can cause mucus to form near your vocal folds. Check herbal remedies for their effect on vocal folds. Don't smoke, and avoid secondhand smoke.

Avoid caffeine and alcohol. Caffeine is dehydrating, and both caffeine and alcohol can activate gastro-esophageal reflux disease (GERD). Avoid eating foods that activate GERD.

Avoid mentholated drops or medicines, as they can dry out your vocal folds. If you must take antihistamines, increase your water intake to compensate for dryness.

Keep your drinks at room temperature: not too hot and not iced.

Your Vocal Mechanism

Your vocal cords are tiny muscles residing in the larynx. They aren't much bigger than the nail bed on the pinky finger of your hand. If they get inflamed, it can wreak havoc with their ability to produce a clear tone. Inflamed, enlarged, mucus-covered cords sound like piano strings with cotton wrapped around them, or worse. If you have GERD, your vocal cords could become engorged, and callous-like nodules could form. All of that would cause a different voice quality – hoarseness, for example.

Avoid abusing your vocal mechanism: don't cough excessively, yell, scream, or talk at the end of your exhalation. Breathing at regular intervals avoids straining the vocal cords.

Don't use your voice for extended periods of time without a rest. Even the best cared-for vocal mechanism will weaken with fatigue and overuse. Then you will be prone to hoarseness or vocal nodules. Take frequent voice breaks throughout the day.

Use diaphragmatic breathing and projection of the voice to increase volume. Don't strain the tiny muscles in and around the vocal mechanism. Use amplification if you will be in large spaces with poor acoustics.

Know your material well. This will help you avoid stress and tension before performances.

Use relaxation warm-ups and gentle vocalizations with an open throat. You can achieve an open throat and better resonance by yawning deeply and feeling the back of your throat open and extended.

When Things Go Wrong and You Wake Up Hoarse

Rest and drink plenty of fluids.

Bundle up before going outside in cold or damp weather.

Give your voice vocal rest. This means *no* talking. Not even a whisper (which is actually worse than talking, because it puts more strain on your vocal cords). If you must speak, try speaking in a lower or higher pitch. Your best recourse is vocal rest.

Drink soothing liquids: tea with honey or slippery elm.

Suck non-mentholated cough drops or hard candy.

If you are still hoarse after one week, see a doctor to rule out strep throat.

Have some chicken soup. It can't hurt.

A Short Warm-up Routine

You can do this daily and before performing.

Reach up high, gently lower your body towards your toes, then gradually raise your body one vertebra at a time. Do this two or three times.

Sit comfortably in a quiet place, feet planted firmly about ten inches apart. Breathe deeply five times, lengthening each exhalation just a little bit. To avoid dizziness, always make the exhalation longer than the inhalation.

Gently bend your neck, breathing out as you relax your head in each of four directions. Don't roll your head. Rolling your head can be harmful to your vertebrae.

Lift your shoulders up to your ears, hold for five seconds, release.

As you exhale, imagine a lovely wave traveling downward through your body from the tip of the topmost hair on your head to the bottom of your feet, through imaginary roots down into the ground. Feel your breath and pulse slowing down.

Yawn. Open your throat and practice reciting the first part of your story in an overly open throat manner. Switch to a tight throat. Switch to optimum open throat. Feel all the muscles around your vocal folds open. Yawn several times. Repeat this exercise again.

Practice counting on one breath while enunciating each sound precisely in an overly exaggerated manner. Keep your body in a relaxed state at all times.

Use acupressure-type hand massage, especially between your thumb and forefinger and in your palms. Relaxation is a key component of producing a good voice. Exercises that relax the body also relax the area surrounding the vocal mechanism as well. The tiny musculature associated with the production of voice is very vulnerable to tension and stress.

Practice the last line of your story in an open throat, relaxed mode. Practice the first line of your story the same way.

Smile. Go on stage. Take in your audience with your eyes. Tell your story. You're ready! ❧

Eep! I Have to Use a Microphone

by Katy Rydell

Don't panic. The microphone is your friend. Repeat: Friend. It's there to help bridge the distance between you and your listeners.

Try to find out in advance what kind of microphone you'll be using. Clip-on mikes are terrific because they let you move freely, but you might want to take a minute to think about what you're going to wear. Lightweight, gossamer skirts that can be dragged down by a heavy battery pack until they lie in a twisted clump around your ankles are probably not a good idea. Something with a belt might be better.

If you use a standing mike, it will restrict your ability to move around the stage. A hand-held mike will restrict the use of one hand. Be prepared. Practice at home. Practice standing in one place while you tell your story. Or, for a hand-held mike, plug an extension cord into the wall, hold the plug in one hand, and practice walking around like that, speaking into the plug. It will give you an idea of what it's like to move about with a cord dangling around your feet. You'll also have the chance to practice your gestures using only one hand.

How far does your mouth have to be from the microphone? There's only one way to tell. Show up early enough so you can do a mike check.

Adjust the height of the microphone so it's comfortable for you.

Sometimes microphones emit a high-pitched whining sound that can drive you and your audience crazy. It's called feedback. It happens when the microphone is placed in front of the speakers and the signal your voice sends into the microphone is duplicated by the signal bouncing back from the speakers to the mike in an ongoing loop. What should you do if that happens? You may need to move the microphone back. You may need to turn the speakers slightly away from the microphone. Experiment with what works. This is one more reason to show up early enough to do a mike check.

Don't blow into microphones; they don't like the moisture in your breath.

While you're learning how to adjust the height of your microphone, locate your microphone's on/off switch. Every mike has one. Learn how to use it. If you're wearing a clip-on mike, remove it, or at least turn it off, before you leave at intermission and go to the rest room. Otherwise the audience will have a treat neither you nor they bargained for.

Like all friends, microphones get more comfortable the longer you're with them. Learn where you need to stand, where you need to put your mouth, how loud you need to speak, and you'll be fine. Even more important, your audience will be happy. They'll be able to hear you. ✿

Storytelling Etiquette

*Compiled by Barbara Griffin,
Olga Loya, Sandra MacLees,
Nancy Schimmel, Harlynne
Geisler, and Kathleen Zundell*

Stories are to share and tell. While we encourage the art of sharing stories, we also want to encourage respect in our community. You deserve respect. Respect other tellers.

A storyteller's personal, family, and original stories are her/his copyrighted property. It is unethical and illegal to tell another person's original, personal, and family stories without the permission of the author/storyteller.

Folklore and folktales are owned by the public, but a specific version told by an individual teller or found in a collection is the teller's or author's copyrighted property. If you like a folktale a storyteller has told, ask that teller for a reference of where it can be found. Research the story by finding other versions, and then tell it your way.

Published literary tales and poetry are copyrighted material. They may be told at informal story swaps, but when you tell another's story in a paid professional setting, you need to request the publisher's/author's permission. You need to research copyright law. When telling anywhere, it is common courtesy to credit the source of your story. Pass stories, share stories, and encourage respect within the storytelling community.

Please feel free to copy this etiquette statement and pass it out or read it at storytelling events. ❧

My Story, Your Story, Whose Story?

by Olga Loya

My story, your story, whose story? The question of who owns what story has been an issue and a struggle in the storytelling community for many years. I belong to a group of storytelling women who have been meeting for at least fifteen years. (We can't quite remember how long.) This subject first came up over ten years ago. How should we handle the problem when we learn that other people are telling our stories? From our discussions, we sat down and wrote that simple statement of Storytelling Etiquette. I think we wrote it more to clarify the issues for ourselves than for any other reason. Then Harlynne Geisler sent the statement to NAPPS (now the NSN) and the Storytelling Etiquette statement took on a life of its own. Now it is everywhere.

Yet, although most people agree with the statement, many people still use other people's stories without permission.

I haven't had the experience of actually hearing someone tell one of my personal stories or my version of a folktale. But I have had friends tell me that they have heard other people tell one of my stories. When I hear that, I always feel so strange. Should I be so possessive of my story? Darn right I should feel that way! I work hard on my stories. It's my blood, my sweat, and my life that go into my stories.

When people ask me about my version of a folktale, I always refer them to sources and suggest that they find a way to make the story their own. I also ask them to give me credit if they are doing a story from my book. Credit is important. It is a way of showing respect for the originator of the story and for the art of storytelling.

One of the worst things that a storyteller can do is to tell someone else's story in the first person, as if it were their own experience. There is a wonderful exchange of trust between the teller and the listener. That trust is destroyed when the storyteller lies to the listener. And make no mistake; it is a lie when a teller tries to pass off someone else's story as his or her own. It is important for us to tell our own stories because that is how we touch each other in the deepest way. When someone breaks that trust, the listener is not going to be so willing to be carried away by a story again.

I think that people tell other people's stories either because of naiveté or laziness. The naïve ones think "It's everybody's story," or "It's a compliment to the teller if I tell his or her story." The lazy ones don't want to pay their dues. It is much easier for them to tell someone else's story. Then they don't have to do the research and the thinking about the story and the constant messing with it until it is just right. They are in a hurry to go out and be a "storyteller" and make money. What they don't realize is that there is an amazing reward to putting your own story together, to shaping the story into your style and with your own heart. If new tellers just take other people's material, they will never have that sense of triumph and joy in telling their own stories.

In essence, this is all about respect. Respect for the story. Respect for other tellers. Respect for the audience. Respect for ourselves. I think we storytellers need to stop being so polite. There is a general belief that stories belong to everyone. Yes, they do, but not the original stories, and not the folk tale a storyteller has worked very hard on, seeking just the right tone for a character and for the story. When we hear someone telling someone else's story we need to go up to the performer and make it clear that we know it is not their story. It doesn't have to be a hostile interaction. Maybe it could be, "You know, I thought that was so-and-so's story. I don't think I heard you give credit." We need to stand up and protect our stories, our fellow tellers and ourselves. ❧

What You Need To Know About Copyright Law

by Aaron Shepard

Here are the basics for work originally published in the U.S., for anytime up through the year 2018.

1964 or after

Anything with a copyright date in this period is still protected.

1923 to 1963

Anything copyrighted in this period may still be protected, depending on whether the copyright was ever renewed. The only way to find out is to conduct a copyright search. (Get the Copyright Office's Circular 22, "How to Investigate the Copyright Status of a Work.")

1922 or before

Anything published in this period is definitely out of copyright. Fair game. Free and clear.

Many people believe that folktales cannot be copyrighted. It's true that the tale itself is in the public domain, but how the tale is retold belongs to the author. For instance, the author is likely to have named a character, created a dialogue, or modified a plot incident. Original elements such as these are covered by copyright, and for as long as the story is legally protected, you're not supposed to use them.

To avoid problems, work with at least one version that is no longer in copyright and that you can use as your primary source. If that's not possible, you might work with several distinct versions – retellings from different firsthand sources – in order to reconstruct the tale in generic form. ❦

Excerpted from *The Business of Writing for Children* by Aaron Shepard, Shepard Publications, 1999. Also available at www.aaronshep.com/storytelling

The ABC's of Storytelling

by Yvonne Young

Allow yourself to tell a story you don't think is perfect yet.
Appear to be calm and confident.
Ask for advice when you need it.

Begin with one story.
Believe in yourself and your story.
Breathe deeply from your diaphragm.

Capture the attention of your audience.
Collect stories.
Communicate through stories.

Deliver in dialects only if they are authentic and consistent,
and you're certain no one will be offended.
Discipline with eye contact.
Discover the best way for you to learn a story.

Eliminate unnecessary gestures.
Enliven your stories with energy.
Evaluate stories for ease in learning and telling.

Figure out ways to get feedback.
Find wonderful material in folklore.
Forget about forgetting: you won't if you know your story
so well it's part of you.

Gain confidence by telling as often as you can.
Gather with other storytellers to listen and share.
Gesture when it improves your story.

H abitually rehearse your stories before you tell.
Heighten suspense with appropriate pauses.
Hook your audience with your introduction.

I dentify with your characters.
Imagine your story: see it happening as you tell it.
Improvise if you make a mistake; your audience will probably never know the difference.

J oin your audience in sharing the joy of the story.
Just be yourself; you'll find your natural style.
Journey into the world of storytelling: after a few successes you'll never want to stop.

K eep records of stories you've learned and want to learn.
Kindle your listeners' imaginations and emotions.
Know your story inside and out.

L earn only stories you love.
Let the story speak for itself – don't try to explain it.
Listen to as many stories as possible.

M emorize only the beginning and the end of your stories, and essential key phrases.
Make eye contact with your audience, so each listener feels the story is a personal gift from you.
Match your material to the audience.

N ote changes you want to make after a performance.
Notice audience reactions.
Nurture yourself and your audience with stories that speak to the meaning of life.

O btain permission to tell stories written by other tellers.
Observe what makes other tellers successful.
Outline the story structure.

P articipate with your audience by encouraging them to join in on repeated patterns.
Pause to intensify the meaning and heighten suspense.
Practice your stories orally until they are a part of you.

Qualify yourself with adequate practice and preparation.
Quiet your qualms.
Quit worrying.

Read as many stories as possible.
Retell a new story as often as possible.
Research the background and culture of your stories.

Search out stories with heroines.
Select stories carefully; sometimes they'll select you.
Speak clearly and distinctly.

Tell every chance you get, when you're working on new material.
Try alternatives for characterization and presentation.
Turn mistakes into learning.

Understand your stories thoroughly.
Use a mirror to practice gestures, and a tape recorder to evaluate your telling.
Utilize material from many sources.

Vary your expression with vocal techniques.
Visualize the characters, settings, and action as you tell.
Validate yourself for a story well told!

Warm up your voice to make it more resonant and free.
Wear comfortable clothing.
Widen your horizons with tales from various cultures.

X-cite children about reading and literature through stories.
X-plore to find the best stories for you.
X-press yourself clearly.

Yawn to relax jaw muscles and release tensions before you tell.
Yield to stories: if you keep remembering a particular story, it may be trying to tell you to learn it.

Zest, Zeal, and Zip give life to your stories, to you, and to your audience. ❦

Adapted from an article orginally published in Yarnspinner, November 1989.

Storyteller's Bookshelf

by Judy Sima

Beginners' Quick-Start Library

Cole, Joanna. *Best-Loved Folktales of the World*. Doubleday. 1982.

> 200 tales arranged by regions of the world: east and west Europe, the British Isles, Middle East, Asia, Africa, North and South America, the Caribbean, and the Pacific. Index in the back lists stories by categories: especially good for young children; humorous tales; legends; tales with a moral; witches, ogresses and female monsters; trickster-heroes; married couples, and others.

Davis, Donald. *Telling Your Own Stories: For Family and Classroom Storytelling, Public Speaking, and Personal Journaling*. August House. 1993.

> A small book packed full of "story starters" and memory joggers (interview techniques to help stimulate a person's recollections). Ideas on telling personal stories and building plot, story structure, crisis development, and more.

MacDonald, Margaret Read. *Storyteller's Start-Up Book: Finding, Learning, Performing, and Using Folktales*. August House. 1993.

> Basic start-up information on finding stories, learning to tell the story in one hour, playing and teaching with story, teaching others to tell, and the role of the storyteller. Twenty unusual world folktales are given in short tellable paragraphs.

Mooney, Bill and David Holt. *The Storyteller's Guide: Storytellers Share Advice for the Classroom, Boardroom, Showroom, Podium, Pulpit, and Center Stage.* August House. 1996.

> The authors interviewed over fifty well-known storytelling teachers, librarians, clergymen, actors, musicians, and full-time professional storytellers. Gives opinions and advice on topics such as: shaping stories from printed text; controlling stage fright; marketing; worst performance experiences; learning and rehearsing a story; creating original stories; making a program flow; copyright; using storytelling in the library; recommendations for the "storyteller's bookshelf."

Sawyer, Ruth. *The Way of the Storyteller*. Penguin Books. 1942. 1990.

> A storytelling classic. Sawyer relates her own storytelling journey and vision. An inspiring book for the novice as well as the experienced teller.

Yolen, Jane. *Favorite Folktales from Around the World.* Pantheon. 1988.

> Another "must-have" collection, Yolen presents more than 150 stories from all parts of the world, including stories of ghosts, lovers, tricksters, noodleheads and heroes; tales of wisdom; tall tales; fooling the devil tales; life and death tales; and stories of stories. Also: *Gray Heroes: Elder Tales from Around the World.*

Storytelling Theory and Practice

Bauer, Caroline Feller. *New Handbook for Storytellers: With Stories, Poems, Magic, and More.* American Library Assoc. 1993.

> A practical resource, with over 500 pages of ideas, activities, themes, kinds of stories, multimedia and props, and program development for audiences from preschool children to young adults. Includes decorating and promoting programs; using objects, magic, puppets, poetry, and music; book talks; and book lists for every storytelling idea and theme.

Collins, Rives and Pamela J. Cooper. *The Power of Story: Teaching Through Storytelling.* Prentice Hall. 1996.

> Excellent resource for teachers. Includes the value of telling

stories, choosing and preparing stories, finding your own voice, dramatization, personal narratives, and storytelling activities along with a bibliography and a list of internet sites.

Dailey, Sheila. ***Putting the World in a Nutshell: The Art of the Formula Tale.*** Wilson. 1994.

Easy-to-learn stories following set patterns, such as the chain story, cumulative tale, circle story, endless tale, the story with a problem to solve, and the catch story. Includes explanations and book lists. Useful for creating your own stories.

Hamilton, Martha and Mitch Weiss. ***Children Tell Stories: A Teaching Guide.*** Richard Owen. 1990.

Useful for beginning adults as well as children. How to choose and learn stories, gestures, facial expressions, etc., plus thirty stories from starter stories to most challenging. Also: ***How & Why Stories: World Tales Kids Can Read and Tell.***

Lipman, Doug. ***Improving Your Storytelling: Beyond the Basics for All Who Tell Stories in Work or Play.*** August House. 1999.

Comments on use of language, the senses, kinesthetic imagery, voice, discovering the meaning and structure of your story, when to memorize, benefits of having a rehearsal buddy, the relationship between teller and listener, how to deal with anxiety, how to plan programs.

MacDonald, Margaret Read. ***The Parent's Guide to Storytelling: How to Make Up New Stories and Retell Old Favorites.*** August House. 2001.

Contains ideas for making storytelling easy, spontaneous and affirming. Focuses on storytelling for the youngest listeners, bedtime stories, expandable tales, scary stories, improvisational ideas, and family folklore. Texts of twenty-one stories, with hints on how to tell them.

Maguire, Jack. ***Creative Storytelling: Choosing, Inventing, & Sharing Tales for Children.*** Yellow Moon Press. 1991.

A comprehensive, step-by-step guide to telling stories. Includes information on sources; types of stories; how to gear stories toward children of different ages and interests; techniques for remembering and adapting stories; how to use personal experiences to create new stories; how storytelling leads to other creative activities; creating stories that foster environmental awareness.

Maguire, Jack. *The Power of Personal Storytelling: Spinning Tales to Connect with Others.* Penguin Putnam. 1998.

Step-by-step instructions to develop realistic stories for all tellers, "whether you're a teacher or a salesman, a minister or a parent."

Mellon, Nancy. *Storytelling & The Art of Imagination.* Yellow Moon Press. 2003.

A classic in the field of storytelling as a healing art. Describes how to tap into creative wisdom within the archetypal characters, landscapes and plots found in tales throughout the world. Discussion of how to use the rhythms of voice and speech, visualization, and the imaginative wealth of symbolism to inform the healing imagination.

Schimmel, Nancy. *Just Enough to Make a Story: A Sourcebook for Storytelling.* Sisters' Choice Press. 1992.

Ideas for choosing and using stories in various settings. Includes five stories, annotated book lists, and helpful advice on how to tell stories.

Sima, Judy and Kevin Cordi. *Raising Voices: Youth Storytelling Groups and Troupes.* Libraries Unlimited. 2003.

Step-by-step guide for organizing and running student storytelling clubs including activities, story learning process, coaching, fund raising. Annotated list of resources.

Simmons, Annette. *The Story Factor: Inspiration, Influence, and Persuasion Through the Art of Storytelling.* Perseus Publishing. 2002.

How to tell the "six stories you need to know how to tell" to be persuasive in business. She points out "what Story can do that facts can't," and gives a list of do's and don'ts. Introduction by Doug Lipman.

Weissman, Annie. *Do Tell! Storytelling for You and Your Students.* Linworth Publishing, Inc. 2002.

Succinct introduction for teachers on choosing, learning and telling folktales. Includes lesson plans for integrating storytelling into school subjects, techniques for teaching children to tell, and the full text of thirty-three easy-to-learn public domain tales. Useful bibliographies and a list of internet sites.

Storytelling Collections and Anthologies

Baltuck, Naomi. *Crazy Gibberish and Other Story Hour Stretches (from a Storyteller's Bag of Tricks)*. Linnet Books. 1993. Includes book and cassette.

Chants, short audience participation stories, action songs, musical games, jokes, tongue twisters plus section on how to use the story stretchers and how to create and adapt your own. Also: *Apples from Heaven: Multicultural Folk Tales About Stories and Storytellers.*

Caduto, Michael J. and Joseph Bruchac. *Keepers of the Earth: Native American Stories and Environmental Activities for Children.* Fulcrum. 1988.

Twenty-three Native American stories about creation, fire, earth, water, seasons, plants, and animals are presented along with discussion questions and activities. Also: *Keepers of the Animals: Native American Stories and Wildlife Activities for Children; Keepers of the Night: Native American Stories and Nocturnal Activities for Children; Earth Tales from Around the World.*

Courlander, Harold and George Herzog. *The Cow-tail Switch and Other West African Stories.* Henry Holt. 1986.

Tales about animals, kings, warriors and hunters, clever and foolish people, good and bad people, and how things came to be. Also by Courlander: *People of the Short Blue Corn: Tales and Legends of the Hopi Indians* and *The Tiger's Whisker and Other Tales from Asia and the Pacific*; by Courlander and Wolf Leslau: *The Fire on the Mountain and Other Stories from Ethiopia and Eritrea.*

Cox, Allison and David Albert. *The Healing Heart ~ Families: Storytelling to Encourage Caring and Healthy Families* and *The Healing Heart ~ Communities: Storytelling to Encourage Strong and Healthy Communities.* New Society Publishers. 2003.

These books connect storytelling with mental and social health issues, including adoption, grief, community-building, violence prevention, domestic violence, substance abuse, racism, and homelessness. Included: folktales, personal stories, and articles; ideas for exercises, games, art, and song; resource lists of stories, books, community agencies, and storytellers working in mental health and social services.

Creeden, Sharon. *Fair Is Fair: World Folktales of Justice.* August House. 1994.

Written by a lawyer who became a storyteller. Folktales are paired with modern examples of justice that parallel the ancient stories. Also: *In Full Bloom: Tales of Women in Their Prime.*

DeSpain, Pleasant. *Thirty-three Multicultural Tales to Tell.* August House. 1993.

Written in a simple, uncomplicated manner, easy enough for kids to tell, but probably should be embellished by adults. Includes stories from Mexico, Korea, Tibet, India, Russia, China, Fiji, Africa, and Japan. Also: *The Books of Nine Lives Series; Twenty-two Splendid Tales to Tell from Around the World; Eleven Turtle Tales: Adventure Tales from Around the World; Eleven Nature Tales: A Multicultural Journey; The Emerald Lizard: Fifteen Latin American Tales to Tell.*

Gersie, Alida. *Earth Tales: Storytelling in Times of Change.* The Merlin Press. 1992.

Insights into the group dynamics of therapeutic storytelling, stories appropriate for therapeutic storytelling, and exercises using art, song, movement, and writing to help groups process the stories.

Goss, Linda and Marian E. Barnes. *Talk That Talk: An Anthology of African-American Storytelling.* Simon and Schuster. 1989.

Contains animal tales and fables, historical stories, sermons, stories of family and home, tales of ghosts and witches, humorous tales, raps, rhythms and rhymes along with commentaries on the tales.

Harrison, Annette. *Easy-To-Tell Stories for Young Children.* National Storytelling Press. 1992.

A varied collection of twelve short tales from many folk traditions. Easy stories to tell to children ages two to eight, with suggestions on when to tell a tale and how to introduce it, hints on gesture and tone of voice, and ideas for follow-up activities.

Holt, David and Bill Mooney, editors. *Ready-To-Tell Tales: Surefire Stories from America's Favorite Storytellers.* August House. 1994.

Forty of the country's most popular professional storytellers contribute stories from around the world for beginning storytellers. Includes "a word about fair use" for storytellers who wish to tell the tales. Telling tips and story sources are given. Also: *More Ready to Tell Tales from Around the World.*

Jacobs, Joseph. *English Fairy Tales.* Dover Dell. 1967.

Reprinted from the 1898 edition, by one of England's most well known folklorists. Many of the forty-three tales are classics: The Three Sillies, Jack and the Beanstalk, Teeny-Tiny, Henny-Penny, The Three Bears, Mr. Fox, Tom Thumb, Lazy Jack, The Three Little Pigs, The Golden Arm. Also: *Celtic Fairy Tales; More Celtic Fairy Tales; Indian Fairy Tales.*

Justice, Jennifer. *The Ghost & I: Scary Stories for Participatory Telling.* Yellow Moon Press. 1992.

Sixteen tales by contemporary storytellers, geared for ages five to fourteen, varying from funny to frightening. Notes for each tale demonstrate how to encourage audience participation.

MacDonald, Margaret Read. *Twenty Tellable Tales: Audience Participation Folktales for the Beginning Storyteller.* Wilson. 1986.

Written in short paragraphs with repetitive lines and phrases, these stories are broken down in an easy, tellable format. The stories are mostly "can't miss" and fun to tell. MacDonald has written other wonderful books of tellable stories including: *Look Back and See: Lively Tales for Gentle Tellers; Peace Tales: World Folktales to Talk About; When the Lights Go Out: Twenty Scary Stories to Tell; Celebrate the World:*

Twenty Tellable Folktales for Multicultural Festivals; Shake-It-Up Tales!: Stories to Sing, Drum, and Act Out.

Meade, Erica Helm. *The Moon in the Well: Wisdom Tales to Transform Your Life, Family and Community.* Open Court Publishing. 2001

> Sixty-five folktales with healing applications drawn from the author's counseling experience, plus a theme index suggesting more stories about similar issues.

Many Voices: True Tales from America's Past. National Storytelling Press. 1995.

> Thirty-six stories arranged chronologically from 1643 to 1989, meant to breathe life into history. The stories describe actual events and people or are based on fictional characters in true-to-life situations. Written by storytellers. Stories about: Abraham Lincoln, Sacagawea, Scott Joplin, Sitting Bull, Rosie the Riveter, as well as ordinary citizens who lived during extraordinary times. Companion volume: *Many Voices Teacher's Guide.*

Miller, Teresa & Norma Livo, editors. *Joining In: An Anthology of Audience Participation Stories & How to Tell Them.* Yellow Moon Press. 1988.

> An anthology of stories by many storytellers. Includes notes for each tale demonstrating how to encourage audience participation.

Pantheon Fairy Tale and Folklore Library. Random House.

> Written by scholars and folklorists. Stories, myths and legends can be reworked and adapted for telling. Includes African, African American, Russian, Norwegian, Swedish, Arabian, British Isles, Grimm's, American Indian, American legends, French, Chinese, Japanese, Yiddish.

Schram, Peninnah. *Jewish Stories One Generation Tells Another.* Jason Aaronson. 1987.

> Sixty-four Jewish folktales collected and re-told by America's best known Jewish storyteller, written in tellable form. Also edited by Schram: *Chosen Tales: Jewish Stories by Jewish Storytellers.*

Sierra, Judy. *Cinderella.* Oryx Press. 1992.

Twenty-five variations on the basic theme of the persecuted heroine who emerges victorious, regardless of the circumstances. Each version, from Asia, Africa, Eastern Europe and North America, is accompanied by an introductory paragraph that discusses the cultural background of the story. Similar titles in the Oryx Multicultural Folktale Series by other authors are: *Tom Thumb; A Knock at the Door; Beauties and Beasts.* Another Oryx book by Sierra: *Multicultural Folktales.*

Untermeyer, Louis. *The Firebringer and Other Great Stories: Fifty-five Legends That Live Forever.* M. Evans and Company. 1968.

Classic myths and legends from around the world including Greek myths, the Bible, Scandinavia, France, Spain, and Great Britain.

Wolkstein, Diane. *The Magic Orange Tree and Other Haitian Folktales.* Schocken. 1978.

Contains twenty-seven unique, sometimes scary folktales and songs from Haiti. A storytelling classic.

World Folklore Series. Libraries Unlimited.

In addition to the tales, each book contains background information, historical overview, beliefs and customs, maps, color photographs of the people, land, and crafts. Includes Balkans, Mexico, Celtic tales, Korea, Australian Aborigines, Finland, India, Ukraine, Nepal, Africa, Kenya, Tlingit, Southeast Asia, and others.

Young, Richard and Judy Dockery. *Favorite Scary Stories of American Children.* August House. 1990.

Each story rated for its "fearfulness" and appropriate age level. All are written to tell easily but can be adapted and expanded to fill one's own personal style. Audio-cassette tapes available. Other August House books: *Classic American Ghost Stories* by Deborah Downer and *Ghost Stories from the American South* by W.K. McNeil.

Publishers and Distributors Specializing in Storytelling Books

August House. P.O. Box 3223; Little Rock, AR 72203-3223.
800-284-8784. www.augusthouse.com

Fulcrum Publishing. 350 Indiana Street, Suite 350; Golden, CO
80401-5093. 800-992-2908. www.fulcrum-resources.com

Highsmith Press. W5527 Highway 106; P.O. Box 800; Fort
Atkinson, WI 53538. 800-558-2110. www.hpress.highsmith.com

Libraries Unlimited. P.O. Box 5007; 88 Post Road West; Westport,
CT 06881. 800-225-5800. www.lu.com

National Storytelling Press. 132 Boone Street; Jonesborough, TN
37659. 800-525-4514. www.storynet.org

Shen's Books. 8625 Hubbard Road; Auburn, CA 95602-7815.
530-888-6776. www.shens.com

Shoe String Press. P.O. Box 657; 2 Linsley Street; North Haven,
CT 06473-2517. 203-239-2702. SSPBooks@aol.com

Yellow Moon Press. P.O. Box 381316; Cambridge, MA 02238.
617-776-2230, 800-497-4385. www.yellowmoon.com

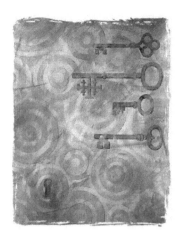

Hotlist of Internet Sites

by Vicky Reed and Karen Chace

The first three sites listed will get you almost anywhere you'd like to go. All three are excellent starting points for links to other resources.

StoryNet

A great resource from National Storytelling Network. Includes the National Storytelling Directory, information on the National Storytelling Festival, the National Storytelling Conference, Tellabration!, and awards, and links to local guilds, state liaisons and educational opportunities. www.storynet.org

Netting Storytelling Resources

Marilyn McPhie's Internet Hotlist on Storytelling. Links to general resources, organizations, festivals, events, tellers, and stories. www.kn.att.com/wired/fil/pages/liststorytelma.html

Storytelling...Tales to Tell

Vicky Reed's Internet Hotlist on Storytelling. Links to Internet resources offering basic information on storytelling, stories to tell, story-based activities, and more. www.kn.att.com/wired/fil/pages/liststorytelvi.html

To give you an idea of the kinds of sites that are out there, here are some examples:

Aaron Shepard's Author Online

Aaron's specialty is retelling folktales and traditional literature from around the world. This is a wonderful collection of folktales, original scripts and articles on how to find, prepare and tell your story. www.aaronshep.com

Folklore and Mythology Electronic Texts

Electronic Texts edited and/or translated by D. L. Ashliman at the University of Pittsburgh. Set up in an A-Z format, this is an extensive list of full texts of stories. www.pitt.edu/ ~ dash/folktexts.html

Story Arts Online

This colorful easy-to-use web site includes storytelling lesson plans, stories, activities tied to the New York State English Language Arts Standards and more. Good resource for short stories and teacher ideas. Created by Heather Forest. www.storyarts.org

Storytell Listserv

Storytell is a free forum service offered by Texas Women's University for discussions about storytelling. It serves as a source of information on conferences, workshops and events as well as a place to ask (and answer) questions about the origins and variations of stories, the business of storytelling, or organization of storytelling events. www.twu.edu/cope/slis/storytell.htm

Tim Sheppard's Storytelling Resources for Storytellers

The Storytelling FAQ (Frequently Asked Questions) section is a great source of basic information for beginners. Annotated links to storytelling resources. Created by Tim Sheppard. www.timsheppard. co.uk/story

Tons-o-Trickster

There are more trickster links here than you could possibly hope to surf in one sitting; anything and everything related to the trickster. http://members.aol.com/pmichaels/glorantha/foolsparadise.html

Winnebago Mythology

Encyclopedia of Hotcâk (Winnebago) Mythology. An extremely comprehensive site for Native American folktales. Includes myths, maps, legends, and an index of stories by subject matter. Created by Richard L. Dieterle at the University of Minnesota. www. hotcakencyclopedia.com

Contributors

Karen Chace has been sharing stories professionally since 2000 and is the founder and director of a student storytelling troupe, producing their Storytelling Festival each year. She is also a contributing author to the National Storytelling Network's second storytelling guide, *Telling Stories to Children*, and writes a regular column on storytelling web sites for *Storytelling Magazine*. Additional websites can be viewed on her Storytelling Links page at www.storybug.net.

Barbara H. Clark is a former librarian for the Los Angeles Public Library. She is an active member of Community Storytellers and the Griot Workshop. She tells stories regularly both as a solo performer and as a member of the performance team, Tellers and Talkers. For six years in a row, the City of Los Angeles Department of Cultural Affairs funded her Artist-in-Residence workshops teaching seniors how to tell their personal stories. bhcstory1@yahoo.com

Gay Ducey is a storyteller, author, teacher, and librarian. She is a recipient of the Oracle Circle of Excellence Award and maintains an active schedule of performing, teaching, and librarianship. She is co-author of *A Crash Course in Storytelling*, described by School Library Journal as "an essential purchase." mducey@earthlink.net

Elizabeth Ellis is a recipient of the John Henry Faulk Award, presented by the Tejas Storytelling Association for significant contributions to storytelling in Texas, and a member of the National Storytelling Network's Circle of Excellence. With Loren Niemi, she is author of *Inviting the Wolf In: Thinking About Difficult Stories.* (August House, 2001.) She is an NEA American Masterpiece Artist. storyellis@sbcglobal.net

Bonnie Greenberg, M. S., is a certified speech-language pathologist, a member of ASHA, and a storyteller. She is the recent co-chair of the National Jewish Storytelling Network, served on the Board of LANES, and is featured in 120 Contemporary Storytellers. She has been featured at museums, festivals, conferences, and on NPR. Her two audiocassettes have won several awards, including a Parent's Choice Award and a NAPPA Gold Award. www.BonnieGreenberg.net

Bill Harley, a Grammy award-winning artist, uses song and story to paint a vibrant and hilarious picture of growing up, schooling and family life. His work spans the generation gap, reminds us of our common humanity, and challenges us to be our very best selves. A prolific author and recording artist, Bill is also a regular commentator for NPR's All Things Considered and featured on PBS. Harley joined the National Storytelling Network's Circle of Excellence in 2001 and tours nationwide as an author and performing artist. www.billharley. com, www.myspace.com/billharleymusic

Olga Loya has performed and taught workshops all over the United States and Mexico. She has three video/books, one audio cassette, and is a story contributor to The Healing Hearts Community book and *More Ready to Tell Tales From Around The World.* She is also author of *Momentos Mágicos/Magic Moments* (August House, 1997), a collection of stories in Spanish and English. Her book won the 1998 Aesop Accolade and the International Reading Association Award for young adults. She has been a featured teller at the First Latin American Storytelling Festival in Guadalajara, Mexico and at the National Storytelling Festival in Jonesborough TN. oloya1@ mindspring.com

Margaret Read MacDonald is a former NSN board member. MacDonald has a Ph.D. in Folklore from Indiana University and over 30 years experience as a children's librarian. She is author of over 50 books on folklore and storytelling, including *The Great Smelly, Slobbery, Small-Tooth Dog* (August House), *Bat's Big Game* (Albert Whitman), *Peace Tales* (August House), and *Ten Traditional*

Tellers (Univ. of Illinois). MacDonald travels the world sharing tales and teaching others to tell. Recent trips included promotions for Chinese, Indonesian, and Japanese editions of her books. www. margaretreadmacdonald.com

Glenn Morrow is the former editor of *Storytelling Magazine* and *The Museletter.* In 2000 he received NSN's Leadership Award for the Northeast. He served on the NSN Board of Directors from 2002 to 2007. A writer of fiction and technical software documentation, he got his storytelling start at Brother Blue's weekly series in Cambridge, Massachusetts, and continues to tell there regularly. morrow@intersystems.com

Caren S. Neile, MFA, Ph. D., directs the South Florida Storytelling Project at Florida Atlantic University in Boca Raton, where she teaches storytelling. She founded the Palm Beach County Storytelling Guild and is founding managing editor of *Storytelling, Self, Society: An Interdisciplinary Journal of Storytelling Studies.* Her numerous publications include the book *Hidden: A Sister and Brother in Nazi Poland,* and she edited a collection of stories by Roslyn Bresnick-Perry. cneile@fau.edu.

Vicky Reed is a Library Media Specialist for the San Diego County Office of Education and for 20 years she has taught storytelling classes in conjunction with an adult storytelling concert series she produces at the University of San Diego. tellreed@aol.com

Katy Rydell started telling stories in 1984. She has taught workshops and classes at CSULA, the University of San Diego, Loyola Marymount University, Dominican College, and the Los Angeles Opera. For fifteen years she was editor and publisher of the quarterly newsletter *STORIES.* In 1994 Houghton Mifflin published her children's book, *Wind Says Good Night.* www.katyrydell.com

Nancy Schimmel of Berkeley, California, has told at numerous conferences, festivals, schools (k-college), libraries, and has taught storytelling in fifth grade through graduate school, including UCLA, University of Wisconsin at Madison, and UC Berkeley. www. sisterschoice.com

Aaron Shepard is the author of many picture books of retold folktales. Readers' theater scripts for many of his stories are available on his website. www.aaronshep.com/storytelling

Judy Sima is an award winning storyteller, educator and widely published author of articles on storytelling. Judy is nationally recognized for her inspiring workshops for educators, librarians, students, and families. Her book, *Raising Voices: Creating Youth Storytelling Groups and Troupes*, coauthored with Kevin Cordi, is a Storytelling World Honor Book and Anne Izard Storyteller's Choice Award winner. Judy@JudySima.com

Karen Wollscheid is a graphic and web designer who also has experience producing storytelling events. She is Business Manager for Northlands Storytelling Network and past Executive Director for Illinois Storytelling, Inc. www.storybizdesign.com

Yvonne Young is a retired elementary teacher who teaches storytelling workshops and designs storytelling assemblies and residencies for Lane Arts Council's Youth Arts Program in Eugene, Oregon. She performs in many venues ranging from festivals and schools to libraries, pre-schools, and adult groups. Yvonne is Oregon State Liaison to the National Storytelling Network. Her DVD, *Two Goats on a Bridge: Stories to Promote Peace and Protect the Planet*, features stories from Margaret Read MacDonald's books *Peace Tales* and *Earth Care*. yey@efn.org